PICNIC, LIGHTNING

PITT POETRY SERIES
Ed Ochester, Editor

PICNIC, LIGHTNING

Billy Collins

UNIVERSITY OF PITTSBURGH PRESS

The publication of this book is supported by a grant from the Pennsylvania Council on the Arts.

Published by the University of Pittsburgh Press, Pittsburgh, Pa. 15261

Manufactured in the United States of America

Printed on acid-free paper

10 9 8 7 6 5

A CIP catalog record for this book is available from the British Library

LIBRARY OF CONGRESS CATALOGING-IN-PUBLICATION DATA
Collins, Billy.
    Picnic, lightning / Billy Collins.
        p.   cm.— (Pitt poetry series)
        ISBN 0-8229-4066-3 (acid-free paper).—
        ISBN 0-8229-5970-5 (pbk. : acid-free paper).
    I Title. II. Series.
    PS3553.O47478P52   1998
    811'. 54—dc21   97-33955

To the memory of Katherine Collins (1901-1997)

Contents

PICNIC, LIGHTNING

"We spend our life trying to bring together in the same instant a ray of sunshine and a free bench."

Beckett, *Texts for Nothing*

A Portrait of the Reader with a Bowl of Cereal

"A poet . . . never speaks directly,
as to someone at the breakfast table."
                                        —*Yeats*

Every morning I sit across from you
at the same small table,
the sun all over the breakfast things—
curve of a blue-and-white pitcher,
a dish of berries—
me in a sweatshirt or robe,
you invisible.

Most days, we are suspended
over a deep pool of silence.
I stare straight through you
or look out the window at the garden,
the powerful sky,
a cloud passing behind a tree.

There is no need to pass the toast,
the pot of jam,
or pour you a cup of tea,
and I can hide behind the paper,
rotate in its drum of calamitous news.

But some days I may notice
a little door swinging open
in the morning air,
and maybe the tea leaves
of some dream will be stuck
to the china slope of the hour—

then I will lean forward,
elbows on the table,
with something to tell you,
and you will look up, as always,
your spoon dripping milk, ready to listen.

I

Fishing on the Susquehanna in July

I have never been fishing on the Susquehanna
or on any river for that matter
to be perfectly honest.

Not in July or any month
have I had the pleasure—if it is a pleasure—
of fishing on the Susquehanna.

I am more likely to be found
in a quiet room like this one—
a painting of a woman on the wall,

a bowl of tangerines on the table—
trying to manufacture the sensation
of fishing on the Susquehanna.

There is little doubt
that others have been fishing
on the Susquehanna,

rowing upstream in a wooden boat,
sliding the oars under the water
then raising them to drip in the light.

But the nearest I have ever come to
fishing on the Susquehanna
was one afternoon in a museum in Philadelphia

when I balanced a little egg of time
in front of a painting
in which that river curled around a bend

under a blue cloud-ruffled sky,
dense trees along the banks,
and a fellow with a red bandanna

sitting in a small, green
flat-bottom boat
holding the thin whip of a pole.

That is something I am unlikely
ever to do, I remember
saying to myself and the person next to me.

Then I blinked and moved on
to other American scenes
of haystacks, water whitening over rocks,

even one of a brown hare
who seemed so wired with alertness
I imagined him springing right out of the frame.

To a Stranger Born in Some Distant Country Hundreds of Years from Now

"I write poems for a stranger who will be born in some
distant country hundreds of years from now."
                                              Mary Oliver

Nobody here likes a wet dog.
No one wants anything to do with a dog
that is wet from being out in the rain
or retrieving a stick from a lake.
Look how she wanders around the crowded pub tonight
going from one person to another
hoping for a pat on the head, a rub behind the ears,
something that could be given with one hand
without even wrinkling the conversation.

But everyone pushes her away,
some with a knee, others with the sole of a boot.
Even the children, who don't realize she is wet
until they go to pet her,
push her away
then wipe their hands on their clothes.
And whenever she heads toward me,
I show her my palm, and she turns aside.

O stranger of the future!
O inconceivable being!
whatever the shape of your house,
however you scoot from place to place,
no matter how strange and colorless the clothes you may wear,
I bet nobody there likes a wet dog either.
I bet everybody in your pub,
even the children, pushes her away.

I Chop Some Parsley While Listening to Art Blakey's Version of "Three Blind Mice"

And I start wondering how they came to be blind.
If it was congenital, they could be brothers and sisters,
and I think of the poor mother
brooding over her sightless young triplets.

Or was it a common accident, all three caught
in a searing explosion, a firework perhaps?
If not,
if each came to his or her blindness separately,

how did they ever manage to find one another?
Would it not be difficult for a blind mouse
to locate even one fellow mouse with vision
let alone two other blind ones?

And how, in their tiny darkness,
could they possibly have run after a farmer's wife
or anyone else's wife for that matter?
Not to mention why.

Just so she could cut off their tails
with a carving knife, is the cynic's answer,
but the thought of them without eyes
and now without tails to trail through the moist grass

or slip around the corner of a baseboard
has the cynic who always lounges within me
up off his couch and at the window
trying to hide the rising softness that he feels.

By now I am on to dicing an onion
which might account for the wet stinging
in my own eyes, though Freddie Hubbard's
mournful trumpet on "Blue Moon,"

which happens to be the next cut,
cannot be said to be making matters any better.

Afternoon with Irish Cows

There were a few dozen who occupied the field
across the road from where we lived,
stepping all day from tuft to tuft,
their big heads down in the soft grass,
though I would sometimes pass a window
and look out to see the field suddenly empty
as if they had taken wing, flown off to another county.

Then later, I would open the blue front door,
and again the field would be full of their munching,
or they would be lying down
on the black and white maps of their sides,
facing in all directions, waiting for rain.
How mysterious, how patient and dumbfounded
they appeared in the long quiet of the afternoons.

But every once in a while, one of them
would let out a sound so phenomenal
that I would put down the paper
or the knife I was cutting an apple with
and walk across the road to the stone wall
to see which one of them was being torched
or pierced through the side with a long spear.

Yes, it sounded like pain until I could see
the noisy one, anchored there on all fours,
her neck outstretched, her bellowing head
laboring upward as she gave voice
to the rising, full-bodied cry
that began in the darkness of her belly
and echoed up through her bowed ribs into her gaping mouth.

Then I knew that she was only announcing
the large, unadulterated cowness of herself,
pouring out the ancient apologia of her kind
to all the green fields and the gray clouds,
to the limestone hills and the inlet of the blue bay,
while she regarded my head and shoulders
above the wall with one wild, shocking eye.

Marginalia

Sometimes the notes are ferocious,
skirmishes against the author
raging along the borders of every page
in tiny black script.
If I could just get my hands on you,
Kierkegaard, or Conor Cruise O'Brien,
they seem to say,
I would bolt the door and beat some logic into your head.

Other comments are more offhand, dismissive—
"Nonsense." "Please!" "HA!!"—
that kind of thing.
I remember once looking up from my reading,
my thumb as a bookmark,
trying to imagine what the person must look like
who wrote "Don't be a ninny"
alongside a paragraph in *The Life of Emily Dickinson*.

Students are more modest
needing to leave only their splayed footprints
along the shore of the page.
One scrawls "Metaphor" next to a stanza of Eliot's.
Another notes the presence of "Irony"
fifty times outside the paragraphs of *A Modest Proposal*.

Or they are fans who cheer from the empty bleachers,
hands cupped around their mouths.
"Absolutely," they shout
to Duns Scotus and James Baldwin.
"Yes." "Bull's-eye." "My man!"
Check marks, asterisks, and exclamation points
rain down along the sidelines.

And if you have managed to graduate from college
without ever having written "Man vs. Nature"
in a margin, perhaps now
is the time to take one step forward.

We have all seized the white perimeter as our own
and reached for a pen if only to show
we did not just laze in an armchair turning pages;
we pressed a thought into the wayside,
planted an impression along the verge.

Even Irish monks in their cold scriptoria
jotted along the borders of the Gospels
brief asides about the pains of copying,
a bird singing near their window,
or the sunlight that illuminated their page—
anonymous men catching a ride into the future
on a vessel more lasting than themselves.

And you have not read Joshua Reynolds,
they say, until you have read him
enwreathed with Blake's furious scribbling.

Yet the one I think of most often,
the one that dangles from me like a locket,
was written in the copy of *Catcher in the Rye*
I borrowed from the local library
one slow, hot summer.
I was just beginning high school then,
reading books on a davenport in my parents' living room,
and I cannot tell you
how vastly my loneliness was deepened,

how poignant and amplified the world before me seemed,
when I found on one page

a few greasy looking smears
and next to them, written in soft pencil—
by a beautiful girl, I could tell,
whom I would never meet—
"Pardon the egg salad stains, but I'm in love."

What I Learned Today

I had never heard of John Bernard Flannagan,
American sculptor,
until I found him on page 961
of the single-volume encyclopedia I am reading
at the rate of one page each day.
He was so poor, according to the entry,
he could not afford the good, quarried marble
and instead had to carve animals
out of the fieldstones he gathered
until he committed suicide in 1942,
the year, I can't help thinking, I turned one.

Of course I know what flannel is,
but that French flannel is napped on only one side
is new to me and a reminder that
no matter what the size the aquarium of one's learning,
another colored pebble can always be dropped in.

Tonight a fog blows by the windows,
and a mist falls through the porch lights
as my index finger descends from flat-coated retriever,
to flatfish, those sideways creatures—
turbot, plaice, flounder, sole—
all swimming through the dark with close-set eyes,
toothless, twisted mouths,
and a preference for warm, shallow water.

But this is nothing new to me.
No dots are connected in the vast grid
of my autodidacticism.
No branch is pruned in the forest of my ignorance,

which is why I am stepping over the Flathead River
of Canada and Montana's Flathead Lake
and coming to rest on the Flathead Indians
who never actually practiced head-flattening,
I am disappointed to learn,
but got their name from neighboring tribes
who shaped the fronts of their own heads
to achieve a pointed appearance,
which is how I hope to look
when the entire contents of this book
press against the inside of my high forehead.

What a relief to emerge
from all this flatheadedness and land on
Flaubert, son of a surgeon, victim of a nervous
disorder, and pursuer of *le mot juste*.
Yet the entry for the supreme master of the realistic novel
is no taller than a filtered cigarette
and hardly half the size of the piscatory word-puff
that envelops the subject of flatfish.

Posterity is, indeed, a cruel and savagely attired mistress,
but my own slow, sentimental education
must continue with the revelation
that while there were three emperors and
a Catholic patriarch all named Flavian,
there is only one Dan Flavin, another sculptor,
who works, the bottom of the narrow column tells me,
in the medium of fluorescent lights,
luminous tubes, strangely configured.

The hour is late as I mark my place
with a playing card and close the book in my lap.
A cool vapor flows over the windowsills.
Appalachia is behind me, Napoleon lies ahead,
and I will save for tomorrow the subject of flax
(the chief source of fiber and seed oil
from prehistoric times to the development of cotton).
It is time to float on the waters of the night.
Time to wrap my arms around this book
and press it to my chest, life preserver
in a sea of unremarkable men and women,
anonymous faces on the street,
a hundred thousand unalphabetized things,
a million forgotten hours.

Journal

Ledger of the head's transactions,
log of the body's voyage,
it rides all day in a raincoat pocket,
ready to admit any droplet of thought,
nut of a maxim,
narrowest squint of an observation.

It goes with me
to a gallery where I open it to record
a note on red and the birthplace of Corot,
into the tube of an airplane
so I can take down the high dictation of clouds,
or on a hike in the woods where a young hawk
might suddenly fly between its covers.

And when my heart is beating
too rapidly in the dark,
I will go downstairs in a robe,
open it up to a blank page,
and try to settle on the blue lines
whatever it is that seems to be the matter.

Net I tow beneath the waves of the day,
giant ball of string or foil,
it holds whatever I uncap my pen to save:
a snippet of Catullus,
a passage from Camus,
a tiny eulogy for the evening anodyne of gin,
a note on what the kingfisher looks like when he swims.

And there is room in the margins
for the pencil to go lazy and daydream
in circles and figure eights,
or produce some illustrations,
like Leonardo in his famous codex—
room for a flying machine,
the action of a funnel,
a nest of pulleys,
and a device that is turned by water,

room for me to draw
a few of my own contraptions,
inventions so original and visionary
that not even I—genius of the new age—
have the slightest idea what they are for.

Some Days

Some days I put the people in their places at the table,
bend their legs at the knees,
if they come with that feature,
and fix them into the tiny wooden chairs.

All afternoon they face one another,
the man in the brown suit,
the woman in the blue dress,
perfectly motionless, perfectly behaved.

But other days, I am the one
who is lifted up by the ribs,
then lowered into the dining room of a dollhouse
to sit with the others at the long table.

Very funny,
but how would you like it
if you never knew from one day to the next
if you were going to spend it

striding around like a vivid god,
your shoulders in the clouds,
or sitting down there amidst the wallpaper,
staring straight ahead with your little plastic face?

Silence

Now it is time to say what you have to say.
The room is quiet.
The whirring fan has been unplugged,
and the girl who was tapping
a pencil on her desktop has been removed.

So tell us what is on your mind.
We want to hear the sound of your foliage,
the unraveling of your tool kit,
your songs of loneliness,
your songs of hurt.

The trains are motionless on the tracks,
the ships at rest in the harbor.
The dogs are cocking their heads
and the gods are peering down from their balloons.
The town is hushed,

and everyone here has a copy.
So tell us about your parents—
your father behind the steering wheel,
your cruel mother at the sink.
Let's hear about all the clouds you saw, all the trees.

Read the poem you brought with you tonight.
The ocean has stopped sloshing around,
and even Beethoven
is sitting up in his deathbed,
his cold hearing-horn inserted in one ear.

Picnic, Lightning

"My very photogenic mother died in a freak accident
(picnic, lightning) when I was three."

Lolita

It is possible to be struck by a meteor
or a single-engine plane
while reading in a chair at home.
Safes drop from rooftops
and flatten the odd pedestrian
mostly within the panels of the comics,
but still, we know it is possible,
as well as the flash of summer lightning,
the thermos toppling over,
spilling out on the grass.

And we know the message
can be delivered from within.
The heart, no valentine,
decides to quit after lunch,
the power shut off like a switch,
or a tiny dark ship is unmoored
into the flow of the body's rivers,
the brain a monastery,
defenseless on the shore.

This is what I think about
when I shovel compost
into a wheelbarrow,
and when I fill the long flower boxes,
then press into rows
the limp roots of red impatiens—

the instant hand of Death
always ready to burst forth
from the sleeve of his voluminous cloak.

Then the soil is full of marvels,
bits of leaf like flakes off a fresco,
red-brown pine needles, a beetle quick
to burrow back under the loam.
Then the wheelbarrow is a wilder blue,
the clouds a brighter white,

and all I hear is the rasp of the steel edge
against a round stone,
the small plants singing
with lifted faces, and the click
of the sundial
as one hour sweeps into the next.

II

In the Room of a Thousand Miles

I like writing about where I am,
where I happen to be sitting,
the humidity or the clouds,
the scene outside the window—
a pink tree in bloom,
a neighbor walking his small, nervous dog.
And if I am drinking
a cup of tea at the time
or a small glass of whiskey,
I will find a line to put it on.

My wife hands these poems back to me
with a sigh.
She thinks I ought to be opening up
my aperture to let in
the wild rhododendrons of Ireland,
the sun-blanched stadiums of Rome,
that waterclock in Bruges—
the world beyond my inkwell.

I tell her I will try again
and travel back to my desk
where the chair is turned to the window.
I think about the furniture of history.
I consider the globe, the lights of its cities.
I visualize a lion rampant on an iron shield,
a quiet battlefield, a granite monument.

And then—just between you and me—
I take a swallow of cold tea
and in the manner of the ancient Chinese

pick up my thin pen
and write down that bird I hear outside,
the one that sings,
pauses,
then sings again.

Morning

Why do we bother with the rest of the day,
the swale of the afternoon,
the sudden dip into evening,

then night with his notorious perfumes,
his many-pointed stars?

This is the best—
throwing off the light covers,
feet on the cold floor,
and buzzing around the house on espresso—

maybe a splash of water on the face,
a palmful of vitamins—
but mostly buzzing around the house on espresso,

dictionary and atlas open on the rug,
the typewriter waiting for the key of the head,
a cello on the radio,

and, if necessary, the windows—
trees fifty, a hundred years old
out there,
heavy clouds on the way
and the lawn steaming like a horse
in the early morning.

Bonsai

All it takes is one to throw a room
completely out of whack.

Over by the window
it looks hundreds of yards away,

a lone stark gesture of wood
on the distant cliff of a table.

Up close, it draws you in,
cuts everything down to its size.

Look at it from the doorway,
and the world dilates and bloats.

The button lying next to it
is now a pearl wheel,

the book of matches is a raft,
and the coffee cup a cistern

to catch the same rain
that moistens its small plot of dark, mossy earth.

For it even carries its own weather,
leaning away from a fierce wind

that somehow blows
through the calm tropics of this room.

The way it bends inland at the elbow
makes me want to inch my way

to the very top of its spiky greenery,
hold onto for dear life

and watch the sea storm rage,
hoping for a tiny whale to appear.

I want to see her plunging forward
through the troughs,

tunneling under the foam and spindrift
on her annual, thousand-mile journey.

Splitting Wood

Frost covered this decades ago,
and frost will cover it again tonight,
the leafy disarray of this woodland

now thinned down to half its trees,
but this morning I stand here
sweating in a thin shirt

as I split a stack of ash logs
into firewood
with two wedges, an ax, and a blue-headed maul.

The pleasures here are well known:
the feet planted wide,
the silent unstoppable flow of the downswing,

the coordination that is called hand-eye,
because the hand achieves
whatever the concupiscent eye desires

when it longs for a certain spot,
which, in this case, is the slightest fissure
visible at one end of the log

where the thin, insinuating edge
of the blade can gain entry,
where the shape of its will can be done.

I want to say there is nothing
like the sudden opening of wood,
but it is like so many other things—

the stroke of the ax like lightning,
the bisection so perfect
the halves fall away from each other

as in a mirror,
and hit the soft ground
like twins shot through the heart.

And rarely, if the wood
accepts the blade without conditions,
the two pieces keep their balance

in spite of the blow,
remain stunned on the block
as if they cannot believe their division,

their sudden separateness.
Still upright, still together,
they wobble slightly

as two lovers, once secretly bound,
might stand revealed,
more naked than ever,

the darkness inside the tree they shared
now instantly exposed to the blunt
light of this clear November day,

all the inner twisting of the grain
that held them blindly
in their augmentation and contortion

now rushed into this brightness
as if by a shutter
that, once opened, can never be closed.

Shoveling Snow with Buddha

In the usual iconography of the temple or the local Wok
you would never see him doing such a thing,
tossing the dry snow over the mountain
of his bare, round shoulder,
his hair tied in a knot,
a model of concentration.

Sitting is more his speed, if that is the word
for what he does, or does not do.

Even the season is wrong for him.
In all his manifestations, is it not warm and slightly humid?
Is this not implied by his serene expression,
that smile so wide it wraps itself around the waist of the universe?

But here we are, working our way down the driveway,
one shovelful at a time.
We toss the light powder into the clear air.
We feel the cold mist on our faces.
And with every heave we disappear
and become lost to each other
in these sudden clouds of our own making,
these fountain-bursts of snow.

This is so much better than a sermon in church,
I say out loud, but Buddha keeps on shoveling.
This is the true religion, the religion of snow,
and sunlight and winter geese barking in the sky,
I say, but he is too busy to hear me.

He has thrown himself into shoveling snow
as if it were the purpose of existence,
as if the sign of a perfect life were a clear driveway
you could back the car down easily
and drive off into the vanities of the world
with a broken heater fan and a song on the radio.

All morning long we work side by side,
me with my commentary
and he inside the generous pocket of his silence,
until the hour is nearly noon
and the snow is piled high all around us;
then, I hear him speak.

After this, he asks,
can we go inside and play cards?

Certainly, I reply, and I will heat some milk
and bring cups of hot chocolate to the table
while you shuffle the deck,
and our boots stand dripping by the door.

Aaah, says the Buddha, lifting his eyes
and leaning for a moment on his shovel
before he drives the thin blade again
deep into the glittering white snow.

I Go Back to the House for a Book

I turn around on the gravel
and go back to the house for a book,
something to read at the doctor's office,
and while I am inside, running the finger
of inquisition along a shelf,

another me that did not bother
to go back to the house for a book
heads out on his own,
rolls down the driveway,
and swings left toward town,

a ghost in his ghost car,
another knot in the string of time,
a good three minutes ahead of me—
a spacing that will now continue
for the rest of my life.

Sometimes I think I see him
a few people in front of me on a line
or getting up from a table
to leave the restaurant just before I do,
slipping into his coat on the way out the door.

But there is no catching him,
no way to slow him down
and put us back in sync,
unless one day he decides to go back
to the house for something,

but I cannot imagine
for the life of me what that might be.
He is out there always before me,
blazing my trail, invisible scout,
hound that pulls me along,

shade I am doomed to follow,
my perfect double,
only bumped an inch into the future,
and not nearly as well-versed as I
in the love poems of Ovid—

I who went back to the house
that fateful winter morning and got the book.

After the Storm

Soft yellow-gray light of early morning,
butter and wool,
the two bedroom windows
still beaded and streaked with rain.

The world calm again, routine with traffic,
after its night of convulsions,
when storm drains closed at the throat,
and trees shook in the wind like the hair of dryads.

In the silent house, its roof still on,
too early for the heat to come whistling up
and the guest room doors still closed,
I am propped up on these pillows,

a gray, moth-eaten cashmere jersey
wrapped around my neck
against the unbroken cold of last night.
I am thinking about the dinner party,

the long table, dark bottles of Merlot,
the odd duck and brussels sprouts,
and how, after midnight,
with all of us sprawled on the couch and floor,

the power suddenly went out
leaving us to feel our way around
in the tenth-century darkness
until we found and lit a stash of candles

then drew the circle of ourselves a little tighter
in this softer hula of lights
that gleamed in mirrors and on rims of glasses
while the shutters banged and the rain lashed down.

A sweet nut of a memory—
but the part that sends me whirring
in little ovals of wonder,
as the leftover clouds break apart

and the sun brightly stripes these walls,
is the part that came later,
hours after we had each carried a candle
up the shadowy staircase and gone to bed.

It was three, maybe four in the morning
when the power surged back on,
and, as if a bookmark
had been inserted into the party

when the lamps went dark,
now all the lights downstairs flared again,
and from the stereo speakers
up through the heat register

into our bedroom and our sleep
blared the sound of Jimmy Reed
singing "Baby What You Want Me to Do"
just where he had left off.

So the party resumed without us,
the room again aglow with a life of its own,
the night air charged
with guitar and harmonica,

until one of us put on slippers,
went down to that blazing, festive emptiness,
and turned everything off.
Then, without lights or music,

even the ghosts of ourselves
had to break up their party,
snub out their cigarettes,
carry their wineglasses to the kitchen,

where they kissed each other good night,
and with nowhere else to go,
floated vaguely upstairs
to lie down beside us in our dark and quiet beds.

Snow

I cannot help noticing how this slow Monk solo
seems to go somehow
with the snow
that is coming down this morning,

how the notes and the spaces accompany
its easy falling
on the geometry of the ground,
on the flagstone path,
the slanted roof,
and the angles of the split rail fence

as if he had imagined a winter scene
as he sat at the piano
late one night at the Five Spot
playing "Ruby My Dear."

Then again, it's the kind of song
that would go easily with rain
or a tumult of leaves,

and for that matter it's a snow
that could attend
an adagio for strings,
the best of the Ronettes,
or George Thorogood and the Destroyers.

It falls so indifferently
into the spacious white parlor of the world,
if I were sitting here reading
in silence,

reading the morning paper
or reading *Being and Nothingness,*
not even letting the spoon
touch the inside of the cup,
I have a feeling
the snow would even go perfectly with that.

Moon

The moon is full tonight
an illustration for sheet music,
an image in Matthew Arnold
glimmering on the English Channel,
or a ghost over a smoldering battlefield
in one of the history plays.

It's as full as it was
in that poem by Coleridge
where he carries his year-old son
into the orchard behind the cottage
and turns the baby's face to the sky
to see for the first time
the earth's bright companion,
something amazing to make his crying seem small.

And if you wanted to follow this example,
tonight would be the night
to carry some tiny creature outside
and introduce him to the moon.

And if your house has no child,
you can always gather into your arms
the sleeping infant of yourself,
as I have done tonight,
and carry him outdoors,
all limp in his tattered blanket,
making sure to steady his lolling head
with the palm of your hand.

And while the wind ruffles the pear trees
in the corner of the orchard
and dark roses wave against a stone wall,
you can turn him on your shoulder
and walk in circles on the lawn
drunk with the light.
You can lift him up into the sky,
your eyes nearly as wide as his,
as the moon climbs high into the night.

Looking West

Just beyond the flower garden at the end of the lawn
the curvature of the earth begins,

sloping down from there
over the length of the country

and the smooth surface of the Pacific
before it continues across the convex rice fields of Asia

and, rising, inclines over Europe
and the bulging, boat-dotted waters of the Atlantic,

finally reaching the other side of the house
where it comes up behind a yellow grove of forsythia

near a dilapidated picnic table,
then passes unerringly under the spot

where I am standing, hands in my pockets,
feet planted firmly on the ground.

This Much I Do Remember

It was after dinner.
You were talking to me across the table
about something or other,
a greyhound you had seen that day
or a song you liked,

and I was looking past you
over your bare shoulder
at the three oranges lying
on the kitchen counter
next to the small electric bean grinder,
which was also orange,
and the orange and white cruets for vinegar and oil.

All of which converged
into a random still life,
so fastened together by the hasp of color,
and so fixed behind the animated
foreground of your
talking and smiling,
gesturing and pouring wine,
and the camber of your shoulders

that I could feel it being painted within me,
brushed on the wall of my skull,
while the tone of your voice
lifted and fell in its flight,
and the three oranges
remained fixed on the counter
the way stars are said
to be fixed in the universe.

Then all the moments of the past
began to line up behind that moment
and all the moments to come
assembled in front of it in a long row,
giving me reason to believe
that this was a moment I had rescued
from the millions that rush out of sight
into a darkness behind the eyes.

Even after I have forgotten what year it is,
my middle name,
and the meaning of money,
I will still carry in my pocket
the small coin of that moment,
minted in the kingdom
that we pace through every day.

Japan

Today I pass the time reading
a favorite haiku,
saying the few words over and over.

It feels like eating
the same small, perfect grape
again and again.

I walk through the house reciting it
and leave its letters falling
through the air of every room.

I stand by the big silence of the piano and say it.
I say it in front of a painting of the sea.
I tap out its rhythm on an empty shelf.

I listen to myself saying it,
then I say it without listening,
then I hear it without saying it.

And when the dog looks up at me,
I kneel down on the floor
and whisper it into each of his long white ears.

It's the one about the one-ton
temple bell
with the moth sleeping on its surface,

and every time I say it, I feel the excruciating
pressure of the moth
on the surface of the iron bell.

When I say it at the window,
the bell is the world
and I am the moth resting there.

When I say it into the mirror,
I am the heavy bell
and the moth is life with its papery wings.

And later, when I say it to you in the dark,
you are the bell,
and I am the tongue of the bell, ringing you,

and the moth has flown
from its line
and moves like a hinge in the air above our bed.

Victoria's Secret

The one in the upper left-hand corner
is giving me a look
that says I know you are here
and I have nothing better to do
for the remainder of human time
than return your persistent but engaging stare.
She is wearing a deeply scalloped
flame-stitch halter top
with padded push-up styling
and easy side-zip tap pants.

The one on the facing page, however,
who looks at me over her bare shoulder,
cannot hide the shadow of annoyance in her brow.
You have interrupted me,
she seems to be saying,
with your coughing and your loud music.
Now please leave me alone;
let me finish whatever it was I was doing
in my organza-trimmed
whisperweight camisole with
keyhole closure and a point d'esprit mesh back.

I wet my thumb and flip the page.
Here, the one who happens to be reclining
in a satin and lace merry widow
with an inset lace-up front,
decorated underwire cups and bodice
with lace ruffles along the bottom
and hook-and-eye closure in the back,
is wearing a slightly contorted expression,

her head thrust back, mouth partially open,
a confusing mixture of pain and surprise
as if she had stepped on a tack
just as I was breaking down
her bedroom door with my shoulder.

Nor does the one directly beneath her
look particularly happy to see me.
She is arching one eyebrow slightly
as if to say, so what if I am wearing nothing
but this stretch panne velvet bodysuit
with a low sweetheart neckline
featuring molded cups and adjustable straps.
Do you have a problem with that?!

The one on the far right is easier to take,
her eyes half-closed
as if she were listening to a medley
of lullabies playing faintly on a music box.
Soon she will drop off to sleep,
her head nestled in the soft crook of her arm,
and later she will wake up in her
Spandex slip dress with the high side slit,
deep scoop neckline, elastic shirring,
and concealed back zip and vent.

But opposite her,
stretched out catlike on a couch
in the warm glow of a paneled library,
is one who wears a distinctly challenging expression,
her face tipped up, exposing

her long neck, her perfectly flared nostrils.
Go ahead, her expression tells me,
take off my satin charmeuse gown
with a sheer, jacquard bodice
decorated with a touch of shimmering Lurex.
Go ahead, fling it into the fireplace.
What do I care, her eyes say, we're all going to hell anyway.

I have other mail to open,
but I cannot help noticing her neighbor
whose eyes are downcast,
her head ever so demurely bowed to the side
as if she were the model who sat for Coreggio
when he painted "The Madonna of St. Jerome,"
only, it became so ungodly hot in Parma
that afternoon, she had to remove
the traditional blue robe
and pose there in his studio
in a beautifully shaped satin teddy
with an embossed V-front,
princess seaming to mold the bodice,
and puckered knit detail.

And occupying the whole facing page
is one who displays that expression
we have come to associate with photographic beauty.
Yes, she is pouting about something,
all lower lip and cheekbone.
Perhaps her ice cream has tumbled
out of its cone onto the parquet floor.
Perhaps she has been waiting all day

for a new sofa to be delivered,
waiting all day in a stretch lace hipster
with lattice edging, satin frog closures,
velvet scrollwork, cuffed ankles,
flare silhouette, and knotted shoulder straps
available in black, champagne, almond,
cinnabar, plum, bronze, mocha,
peach, ivory, caramel, blush, butter, rose, and periwinkle.
It is, of course, impossible to say,
impossible to know what she is thinking,
why her mouth is the shape of petulance.

But this is already too much.
Who has the time to linger on these delicate
lures, these once unmentionable things?
Life is rushing by like a mad, swollen river.
One minute roses are opening in the garden
and the next, snow is flying past my window.
Plus the phone is ringing.
The dog is whining at the door.
Rain is beating on the roof.
And as always there is a list of things I have to do
before the night descends, black and silky,
and the dark hours begin to hurtle by,
before the little doors of the body swing shut
and I ride to sleep, my closed eyes
still burning from all the glossy lights of day.

Musée des Beaux Arts Revisited

As far as mental anguish goes,
the old painters were no fools.
They understood how the mind,
the freakiest dungeon in the castle,
can effortlessly imagine a crab with the face of a priest
or an end table complete with genitals.

And they knew that the truly monstrous
lies not so much in the wildly shocking,
a skeleton spinning a wheel of fire, say,
but in the small prosaic touch
added to a tableau of the hellish,
the detail at the heart of the horrid.

In Bosch's *The Temptation of St. Anthony,*
for instance, how it is not so much
the boar-faced man in the pea-green dress
that frightens, but the white mandolin he carries,
not the hooded corpse in a basket,
but the way the basket is rigged to hang from a bare branch;

how, what must have driven St. Anthony
to the mossy brink of despair
was not the big, angry-looking fish
in the central panel,
the one with the two mouselike creatures
conferring on its tail,
but rather what the fish is wearing:

a kind of pale orange officer's cape
and, over that,

a metal body-helmet secured by silvery wires,
a sensible buckled chin strap,
and, yes, the ultimate test of faith—
the tiny sword that hangs from the thing,
that nightmare carp,
secure in its brown leather scabbard.

Lines Composed Over Three Thousand Miles from Tintern Abbey

I was here before, a long time ago,
and now I am here again
is an observation that occurs in poetry
as frequently as rain occurs in life.

The fellow may be gazing
over an English landscape,
hillsides dotted with sheep,
a row of tall trees topping the downs,

or he could be moping through the shadows
of a dark Bavarian forest,
a wedge of cheese and a volume of fairy tales
tucked into his rucksack.

But the feeling is always the same.
It was better the first time.
This time is not nearly as good.
I'm not feeling as chipper as I did back then.

Something is always missing—
swans, a glint on the surface of a lake,
some minor but essential touch.
Or the quality of things has diminished.

The sky was a deeper, more dimensional blue,
clouds were more cathedral-like,
and water rushed over rock
with greater effervescence.

From our chairs we have watched
the poor author in his waistcoat
as he recalls the dizzying icebergs of childhood
and mills around in a field of weeds.

We have heard the poets long dead
declaim their dying
from a promontory, a riverbank,
next to a haycock, within a copse.

We have listened to their dismay,
the kind that issues from poems
the way water issues forth from hoses,
the way the match always gives its little speech on fire.

And when we put down the book at last,
lean back, close our eyes,
stinging with print,
and slip in the bookmark of sleep,

we will be schooled enough to know
that when we wake up
a little before dinner
things will not be nearly as good as they once were.

Something will be missing
from this long, coffin-shaped room,
the walls and windows now
only two different shades of gray,

the glossy gardenia drooping
in its chipped terra-cotta pot.
And on the floor, shoes, socks,
the browning core of an apple.

Nothing will be as it was
a few hours ago, back in the glorious past
before our naps, back in that Golden Age
that drew to a close sometime shortly after lunch.

Paradelle for Susan

I remember the quick, nervous bird of your love.
I remember the quick, nervous bird of your love.
Always perched on the thinnest, highest branch.
Always perched on the thinnest, highest branch.
Thinnest love, remember the quick branch.
Always nervous, I perched on your highest bird the.

It is time for me to cross the mountain.
It is time for me to cross the mountain.
And find another shore to darken with my pain.
And find another shore to darken with my pain.
Another pain for me to darken the mountain.
And find the time, cross my shore, to with it is to.

The weather warm, the handwriting familiar.
The weather warm, the handwriting familiar.
Your letter flies from my hand into the waters below.
Your letter flies from my hand into the waters below.
The familiar waters below my warm hand.
Into handwriting your weather flies you letter the from the.

I always cross the highest letter, the thinnest bird.
Below the waters of my warm familiar pain,
Another hand to remember your handwriting.
The weather perched for me on the shore.
Quick, your nervous branch flew from love.
Darken the mountain, time and find was my into it was with to to.

NOTE: The paradelle is one of the more demanding French fixed forms, first appearing in the *langue d'oc* love poetry of the eleventh century. It is a poem of four six-line stanzas in which the first and second lines, as well as the third and fourth lines of the first three stanzas, must be identical. The fifth and sixth lines, which traditionally resolve these stanzas, must use *all* the words from the preceding lines and *only* those words. Similarly, the final stanza must use *every* word from *all* the preceding stanzas and *only* those words.

Duck/Rabbit

The lamb may lie down with the lion,
But they will never be as close as this pair
Who share the very lines
Of their existence, whose overlapping is their raison d'être.
How strange and symbiotic the binds
That make one disappear
Whenever the other is spied.
Throw the duck a stare,
And the rabbit hops down his hole.
Give the rabbit the eye,
And the duck waddles off the folio.
Say, these could be our mascots, you and I—
      I could look at you forever
      And never see the two of us together.

Egypt

Alone under the bright swords of sunlight,
alone under the stars,
and nothing to do but circle the pyramids

or walk under the nose of the Sphinx
stopping to listen sometimes
to the sound of stone pressing down on stone.

I put on my boatlike hat in the morning
and enter the marketplace,
but by noon I am home again, lying down on a slab

reading some hieroglyphics
or practicing frontality in front of a mirror,
aiming my hands backwards and forwards.

Whenever a cat appears in a doorway—
her little bell announcing the death of us all—
I bow my head like the others

knowing that there is an asp
for every softly rising breast,
a vial of poison for every swirling ear.

Never mind that in the streets
no woman bothers to look at me
with her enormous, painted fish-eye.

When I cross my arms on my chest
for the final time
and point my toes up at the sky,

I will lie at the bottom of the desert
for a thousand years.
I will wait there until a young archaeologist

comes to dig for me,
unwraps the leathery ball of my head
and sweeps the sand from my face with her delicate brush.

Home Again

The black porcelain lamp
painted with boughs of cherry blossoms
still stands on its end table,
unlit, the little chain untouched,
just the way I left it,

just the way it remained while I was off
leaning into the prow of a boat,
doused with spray, heading for a limestone island,
or sitting at the base of a high Celtic cross
eating a green apple.

While I balanced a pan of hot water on a stone wall
and shaved outside a cottage
overlooking the Irish Sea,
this stack of books, this chair, and paperweight
were utterly still, as they are now.

And you, red box of matches on the floor,
you waited here too, faithful as Penelope,
while I saw the tiny fields
disappear under the wing of my plane,
or swam up and down the flowing Corrib River.

As I lay in a meadow near Ballyvaughan,
ankles crossed, arms behind my head,
watching clouds as they rolled in—
billowing, massive, Atlantic-fresh—

you all held your places in these rooms,
stuck to your knitting,
waited for me to stand here again,
bags at my feet, house key still in hand,
admiring your constancy,
your silent fealty, your steadfast repose.

Lines Lost Among Trees

These are not the lines that came to me
while walking in the woods
with no pen
and nothing to write on anyway.

They are gone forever,
a handful of coins
dropped through the grate of memory,
along with the ingenious mnemonic

I devised to hold them in place—
all gone and forgotten
before I had returned to the clearing of lawn
in back of our quiet house

with its jars jammed with pens,
its notebooks and reams of blank paper,
its desk and soft lamp,
its table and the light from its windows.

So this is my elegy for them,
those six or eight exhalations,
the braided rope of the syntax,
the jazz of the timing,

and the little insight at the end
wagging like the short tail
of a perfectly obedient spaniel
sitting by the door.

This is my envoy to nothing
where I say Go, little poem—
not out into the world of strangers' eyes,
but off to some airy limbo,

home to lost epics,
unremembered names,
and fugitive dreams
such as the one I had last night,

which, like a fantastic city in pencil,
erased itself
in the bright morning air
just as I was waking up.

The Many Faces of Jazz

There's the one where you scrunch up
your features into a look of pained concentration,
every riff a new source of agony,

and there's the look of existential bemusement,
eyebrows lifted, chin upheld by a thumb,
maybe a swizzle stick oscillating in the free hand.

And, of course, for ballads,
you have the languorous droop,
her eyes half-closed, lips slightly parted,
the head lolling back, flower on a stem,
exposing plenty of turtleneck.

There's the everything-but-the-instrument look
on the fellow at the front table,
the one poised to mount the bandstand,
and the classic crazy-man-crazy face,
where the fixed grin joins the menacing stare,
especially suitable for long drum solos.

And let us not overlook the empathetic
grimace of the listener
who has somehow located the body
of cold rage dammed up behind the playing
and immersed himself deeply in it.

As far as my own jazz face goes—
and don't tell me you don't have one—
it hasn't changed that much

since its debut in 1957.
It's nothing special, easy enough to spot
in a corner of any club on any given night.
You know it—the reptilian squint,
lips pursed, jaw clenched tight,
and, most essential, the whole
head furiously, yet almost imperceptibly
nodding
in total and absolute agreement.

Taking Off Emily Dickinson's Clothes

First, her tippet made of tulle,
easily lifted off her shoulders and laid
on the back of a wooden chair.

And her bonnet,
the bow undone with a light forward pull.

Then the long white dress, a more
complicated matter with mother-of-pearl
buttons down the back,
so tiny and numerous that it takes forever
before my hands can part the fabric,
like a swimmer's dividing water,
and slip inside.

You will want to know
that she was standing
by an open window in an upstairs bedroom,
motionless, a little wide-eyed,
looking out at the orchard below,
the white dress puddled at her feet
on the wide-board, hardwood floor.

The complexity of women's undergarments
in nineteenth-century America
is not to be waved off,
and I proceeded like a polar explorer
through clips, clasps, and moorings,
catches, straps, and whalebone stays,
sailing toward the iceberg of her nakedness.

Later, I wrote in a notebook
it was like riding a swan into the night,
but, of course, I cannot tell you everything—
the way she closed her eyes to the orchard,
how her hair tumbled free of its pins,
how there were sudden dashes
whenever we spoke.

What I can tell you is
it was terribly quiet in Amherst
that Sabbath afternoon,
nothing but a carriage passing the house,
a fly buzzing in a windowpane.

So I could plainly hear her inhale
when I undid the very top
hook-and-eye fastener of her corset

and I could hear her sigh when finally it was unloosed,
the way some readers sigh when they realize
that Hope has feathers,
that reason is a plank,
that life is a loaded gun
that looks right at you with a yellow eye.

IV

The Night House

Every day the body works in the fields of the world
mending a stone wall
or swinging a sickle through the tall grass—
the grass of civics, the grass of money—
and every night the body curls around itself
and listens for the soft bells of sleep.

But the heart is restless and rises
from the body in the middle of the night,
leaves the trapezoidal bedroom
with its thick, pictureless walls
to sit by herself at the kitchen table
and heat some milk in a pan.

And the mind gets up too, puts on a robe
and goes downstairs, lights a cigarette,
and opens a book on engineering.
Even the conscience awakens
and roams from room to room in the dark,
darting away from every mirror like a strange fish.

And the soul is up on the roof
in her nightdress, straddling the ridge,
singing a song about the wildness of the sea
until the first rip of pink appears in the sky.
Then, they all will return to the sleeping body
the way a flock of birds settles back into a tree,

resuming their daily colloquy,
talking to each other or themselves

even through the heat of the long afternoons.
Which is why the body—that house of voices—
sometimes puts down its metal tongs, its needle, or its pen
to stare into the distance,

to listen to all its names being called
before bending again to its labor.

The Death of the Hat

Once every man wore a hat.

In the ashen newsreels,
the avenues of cities
are broad rivers flowing with hats.

The ballparks swelled
with thousands of strawhats,
brims and bands,
rows of men smoking
and cheering in shirtsleeves.

Hats were the law.
They went without saying.
You noticed a man without a hat in a crowd.

You bought them from Adams or Dobbs
who branded your initials in gold
on the inside band.

Trolleys crisscrossed the city.
Steamships sailed in and out of the harbor.
Men with hats gathered on the docks.

There was a person to block your hat
and a hatcheck girl to mind it
while you had a drink
or ate a steak with peas and a baked potato.
In your office stood a hat rack.

The day war was declared
everyone in the street was wearing a hat.
And they were wearing hats
when a ship loaded with men sank in the icy sea.

My father wore one to work every day
and returned home
carrying the evening paper,
the winter chill radiating from his overcoat.

But today we go bareheaded
into the winter streets,
stand hatless on frozen platforms.

Today the mailboxes on the roadside
and the spruce trees behind the house
wear cold white hats of snow.

Mice scurry from the stone walls at night
in their thin fur hats
to eat the birdseed that has spilled.

And now my father, after a life of work,
wears a hat of earth,
and on top of that,
a lighter one of cloud and sky—a hat of wind.

The List of Ancient Pastimes

First must have come listening
to the wind or regarding
the movements of animals,
then monitoring the stars

and sometime after that
scrutinizing fire;
but somewhere in there belongs
watching the progress of a river

from an elevated bank,
studying the pooling near the edges,
the way the smooth or rippled
current divulges the secret

contours of the unseen bottom,
and the effects of sky-light
on the surface,
all the elongated colors of the flow.

Today it is my turn on the shore.
I flatten the tall grass with my pacing.
I lock my elbows and lean back
listening to the liquid rush.

I scribble in a notebook,
drink from a bottle of water.
I find a perfect stone
and fling it out into the middle.

And sometimes I see something
being carried down,
a cracked-off branch, a bucket on its side
in the late afternoon,

or as the dusk gets heavy,
the head of Orpheus bobbing along,
singing softly
to the overhanging trees,

or the body of Ophelia
held up by her voluminous,
outspread clothes—
the light so faint now

it is difficult to tell
if the red and yellow petals
are embroidered into her gown
or real, floating on the darkness of the water.

Passengers

At the gate, I sit in a row of blue seats
with the possible company of my death,
this sprawling miscellany of people—
carry-on bags and paperbacks—

that could be gathered in a flash
into a band of pilgrims on the last open road.
Not that I think
if our plane crumpled into a mountain

we would all ascend together,
holding hands like a ring of skydivers,
into a sudden gasp of brightness,
or that there would be some common place

for us to reunite to jubilize the moment,
some spaceless, pillarless Greece
where we could, at the count of three,
toss our ashes into the sunny air.

It's just that the way that man has his briefcase
so carefully arranged,
the way that girl is cooling her tea,
and the flow of the comb that woman

passes through her daughter's hair . . .
and when you consider the altitude,
the secret parts of the engines,
and all the hard water and the deep canyons below . . .

well, I just think it would be good if one of us
maybe stood up and said a few words,
or, so as not to involve the police,
at least quietly wrote something down.

Serpentine

This morning I saw suddenly
on the road ahead of me
the moving question mark of a snake,
black thumb of a head lifted,
some ancient node within the dark hood
urging the long thin body forward,
sensing its way
through its slippery existence
as it had been doing since birth,
slithering toward our moment of intersection,
its swishing passage no longer hidden by grass
or the wet cover of leaves,
but its entire length visible now
in the pure daylight of this dilated second,

just as I had been moving toward it, too,
all my life,
in my own upright, warm-blooded way,
walking the long sidewalks, riding trains,
leaning on the railing of a ferry,
or, as today, driving a country road,
which from the air would look like a snake itself
curling through the dense green woods.

No moment was given there
spacious enough
to brake or swerve within,
only time enough to keep my line,
hoping without hope,
knowing, as I needled through the instant,
that the two of us had always been meant to meet here,

my curved line crossing his
as on some unknowable graph
spread out on a vast table
under the glare of a hanging lamp—
a relentless diagram,
millions of faint red lines
forming millions of tiny squares.

Reincarnation and You

To come back at all would be outlandish enough,
let alone to return as something else,
yet most are quick with a preference

for animals, usually, birds
fluttering at the top of the list
pursued by jaguars and cheetahs,

sometimes a peacock
but never an ant, never a snail,
despite the quiet modesty of their lives.

Once around is enough for me
though whenever you ask
I come up with something, a waterfall

or the ferns quivering in its spray.
An enormous piano, I will say one day,
and the next a puddle in a sunny

tropical village after a week of rain.
Or I will pick a lime for the fun of it
and hang there all day in the Florida sun

trying to make death appear as easy
as you make it sound
when you stand by the pearl gray windows

and explain your life as the lapdog of a duchess.
But never mind all that,
never mind the elephant-headed god

and the transmigration of souls.
Forget the rings of time
and the abandonment of desire.

Come closer. Look me in the eye.
Tell me what kind
of animal you want to be today,

and I will whisper in your ear
what I really want to be, come to think of it,
now that all the sun has drained

out of this room and neither one of us
has thought to put on a lamp—
a zoo in a lost city,

one that can be entered or left
only by crossing a range of mountains
covered with deep snow, all year round.

Jazz and Nature

It was another clear sunny morning,
a dry breeze agitating the trees around the house,
and I had nothing on tap—
my usual scene in late August.

I was reading the autobiography
of Art Pepper, so I put on an Art Pepper album
and switched on the outdoor speakers
so I could sit outside in the hot sun,

and read more about his life of junk and prison
while I listened to his speedy, mellow alto
pouring out of two big maples
as if West Coast jazz were the music of Nature itself.

In this way, I drew a kind of box
around the morning,
in three dimensions and in pencil
with me inside it holding a ruler in my hand.

I read and listened and read
and sometimes flipped to the photographs
to check the face of the man
who told me he once drove a greenish gold Cadillac

that you could see forever into, like looking into a lake;
the man who said he composed
a ballad called "Diane" for his second wife
only to realize later

that the tune was way too beautiful for her.
The fellow who admitted to selling
his dog, a champagne poodle named Bijou,
for a twenty-dollar score

and who mentioned that men in prison
who were trying to kick would tuck
their pant legs into their socks
so the slightest breeze would not touch their skin.

Behind where I was sitting in the sun
was an outbreak of wild pink phlox,
and some of the bees nuzzling there
started to hum around my head.

One bee in particular seemed so curious
about me I took a swipe at him,
stood up suddenly and said "Don't mess with me
and I won't mess with you, you little punk,"

a remark no doubt inspired
by my reading about California lowlife
in nineteen fifty-seven,
my all-time favorite year for jazz, as it happens.

But he persisted, this bee, and finally
drove me inside to the cool, dark study
where a cat was sleeping on a chair,
a good place to write this down

and wonder what the rest of the day would hold—
maybe hanging a print on the wall
or getting a surprise phone call
from someone I used to love.

How about some Dexter Gordon
around the cocktail hour,
and who knows?
perhaps an encounter with a vicious ant—

all likely parts of my own autobiography,
a more cautious tale, told in the present tense,
with a few crude illustrations
and a diagram of a small family tree,

the work whose pages are turned
every day like a wheel that is turned by water,
the thing I can never stop writing,
the only book I can never put down.

And His Sextet

Now that all the twilight has seeped
out of the room
and I am alone here listening,

the bass is beginning to sound
like my father
ascending the flights of stairs

every weekday evening,
always the same cadence,
a beat you could build a city on.

And the alto is the woman
I sat next to on a train
who wore a tiny silver watch around her wrist.

The drums are drops of water
on my forehead,
one for every inhabitant of China.

And the tenor, let us say,
is someone's younger brother
who moved out West and never writes,

or the tenor is a pair of aces
lost in the desert,
a black valentine,

or a swan passing under a willow.
But the piano—
the piano is the piano

you gave me one Christmas,
a big black curve
standing at the end of the room

with a red bow tied around its leg
and snow falling on the house
and the row of hemlocks.

And though by now I know some chords
and a few standards,
I still love lying on the floor

like this, eyes closed,
hands behind my head,
pouring forth the solo on "Out of the Blue"

in the Fantasy Studios,
Berkeley, California,
on October 4th, 1951.

Where I Live

The house sits at one end of a two-acre trapezoid.
There is a wide lawn, a long brick path,
rhododendrons, and large, heavy maples.

Behind the geometry of the nine rooms,
the woods run up a hillside;
and across the road in front

is a stream called the Plum Brook.
It must have flowed through an orchard
that no longer exists.

Tomorrow early, I will drive down
and talk to the stonecutter,
but today I am staying home,

standing at one window, then another,
or putting on a jacket
and wandering around outside

or sitting in a chair
watching the trees full of light-green buds
under the low hood of the sky.

This is the first good rain to fall
since my father was buried last week,
and even though he was very old,

I am amazed at how the small drops
stream down the panes of glass,
as usual,

gathering,
as they always have,
in pools on the ground.

My Life

Sometimes I see it as a straight line
drawn with a pencil and a ruler
transecting the circle of the world

or as a finger piercing
a smoke ring, casual, inquisitive,

but then the sun will come out
or the phone will ring
and I will cease to wonder

if it is one thing,
a large ball of air and memory,
or many things,
a string of small farming towns,
a dark road winding through them.

Let us say it is a field
I have been hoeing every day,
hoeing and singing,
then going to sleep in one of its furrows,

or now that it is more than half over,
a partially open door,
rain dripping from the eaves.

Like yours, it could be anything,
a nest with one egg,
a hallway that leads to a thousand rooms—
whatever happens to float into view
when I close my eyes

or look out a window
for more than a few minutes,
so that some days I think
it must be everything and nothing at once.

But this morning, sitting up in bed,
wearing my black sweater and my glasses,
the curtains drawn and the windows up,

I am a lake, my poem is an empty boat,
and my life is the breeze that blows
through the whole scene

stirring everything it touches—
the surface of the water, the limp sail,
even the heavy, leafy trees along the shore.

Aristotle

This is the beginning.
Almost anything can happen.
This is where you find
the creation of light, a fish wriggling onto land,
the first word of *Paradise Lost* on an empty page.
Think of an egg, the letter *A,*
a woman ironing on a bare stage
as the heavy curtain rises.
This is the very beginning.
The first-person narrator introduces himself,
tells us about his lineage.
The mezzo-soprano stands in the wings.
Here the climbers are studying a map
or pulling on their long woolen socks.
This is early on, years before the Ark, dawn.
The profile of an animal is being smeared
on the wall of a cave,
and you have not yet learned to crawl.
This is the opening, the gambit,
a pawn moving forward an inch.
This is your first night with her,
your first night without her.
This is the first part
where the wheels begin to turn,
where the elevator begins its ascent,
before the doors lurch apart.

This is the middle.
Things have had time to get complicated,
messy, really. Nothing is simple anymore.
Cities have sprouted up along the rivers

teeming with people at cross-purposes—
a million schemes, a million wild looks.
Disappointment unshoulders his knapsack
here and pitches his ragged tent.
This is the sticky part where the plot congeals,
where the action suddenly reverses
or swerves off in an outrageous direction.
Here the narrator devotes a long paragraph
to why Miriam does not want Edward's child.
Someone hides a letter under a pillow.
Here the aria rises to a pitch,
a song of betrayal, salted with revenge.
And the climbing party is stuck on a ledge
halfway up the mountain.
This is the bridge, the painful modulation.
This is the thick of things.
So much is crowded into the middle—
the guitars of Spain, piles of ripe avocados,
Russian uniforms, noisy parties,
lakeside kisses, arguments heard through a wall—
too much to name, too much to think about.

And this is the end,
the car running out of road,
the river losing its name in an ocean,
the long nose of the photographed horse
touching the white electronic line.
This is the colophon, the last elephant in the parade,
the empty wheelchair,
and pigeons floating down in the evening.

Here the stage is littered with bodies,
the narrator leads the characters to their cells,
and the climbers are in their graves.
It is me hitting the period
and you closing the book.
It is Sylvia Plath in the kitchen
and St. Clement with an anchor around his neck.
This is the final bit
thinning away to nothing.
This is the end, according to Aristotle,
what we have all been waiting for,
what everything comes down to,
the destination we cannot help imagining,
a streak of light in the sky,
a hat on a peg, and outside the cabin, falling leaves.

Acknowledgments

Grateful acknowledgments are due to the editors of the following publications where many of these poems first appeared: *The American Poetry Review* ("Shoveling Snow with Buddha"); *The American Scholar* ("Duck/Rabbit," "Paradelle for Susan"); *The Berkeley Poetry Review* ("Afternoon with Irish Cows"); *Black Warrior Review* ("I Chop Some Parsley While Listening to Art Blakey's Version of 'Three Blind Mice'"); *Brilliant Corners* ("And His Sextet," "Snow"); *Crab Orchard Review* ("Journal"); *DoubleTake* ("Jazz and Nature"); *Field* ("Some Days," "Silence"); *Five Points* ("Fishing on the Susquehanna in July"); *The Georgia Review* ("Japan," "Bonsai"); *The Kenyon Review* ("The Night House"); *The New England Review* ("Reincarnation and You"); *The Paris Review* ("Aristotle," "Picnic, Lightning," "Musée des Beaux Arts Revisited"); *Plum Review* ("After the Storm," "The Death of the Hat," "The List of Ancient Pastimes," "Moon," "This Much I Do Remember"); *Poetry* ("I Go Back to the House for a Book," "In the Room of a Thousand Miles," "Lines Composed Over Three Thousand Miles from Tintern Abbey," "Lines Lost Among Trees," "Marginalia," "Morning," "My Life," "Serpentine," "Splitting Wood," "What I Learned Today"); *Poetry East* ("Looking West"); *Poetry International* ("Home Again"); *Western Humanities Review* ("Victoria's Secret"); *Wordsmith* ("Where I Live").

"Lines Lost Among Trees" appeared in *The Best American Poetry 1997,* edited by James Tate.

"Japan" appeared in *The 1997 Pushcart Prize XXI.*

A grant from the Research Foundation of The City University of New York facilitated the preparation of this book.

photo: JoAnn Carney

About the Author

Billy Collins is professor of English at Lehman College of the City
University of New York. His poems have appeared in *The New Yorker,
Paris Review, Poetry, American Poetry Review, American Scholar, Harper's,*
and many other magazines. He is the recipient of fellowships from
the National Endowment for the Arts and the Guggenheim Founda-
tion, among others. *Questions About Angels* was a winner of the
National Poetry Series publication prize. *Picnic, Lightning* is his sixth
collection of poetry. He lives in Somers, New York.